Stars!

Story by Pamela Rushby

Illustrations by Luna Valentine

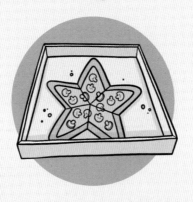

Stars!

Text: Pamela Rushby
Publishers: Tania Mazzeo and Eliza Webb
Series consultant: Amanda Sutera
  Hands on Heads Consulting
Editor: Sarah Layton
Project editor: Annabel Smith
Designer: Jess Kelly
Project designer: Danielle Maccarone
Illustrations: Luna Valentine
Production controller: Renee Tome

NovaStar

Text © 2024 Cengage Learning Australia Pty Limited
Illustrations © 2024 Cengage Learning Australia Pty Limited

ISBN 978 0 17 033384 9

Cengage Learning Australia
Level 5, 80 Dorcas Street
Southbank VIC 3006 Australia
Phone: 1300 790 853
Email: aust.nelsonprimary@cengage.com

For learning solutions, visit **cengage.com.au**

Printed in China by 1010 Printing International Ltd
1 2 3 4 5 6 7 28 27 26 25 24

*Nelson acknowledges the Traditional Owners and Custodians
of the lands of all First Nations Peoples. We pay respect
to Elders past and present, and extend that respect to
all First Nations Peoples today.*

Contents

Chapter 1

Bad News

When Toby's class arrived at school on Friday morning, their teacher, Ms Tan, had bad news. There had been a lot of rain. Roads were flooded, and towns were cut off.

"And the town out west where we were going for our school camp next week is one of them. So I'm afraid camp is cancelled," said Ms Tan. "I'm very sorry. I know you're all disappointed."

The class was not just disappointed. They were *miserable*.

Toby and his class had been looking forward to adventures like sleeping in tents, going hiking, and singing around campfires. They had especially been looking forward to learning all about stars and planets.

Toby thought about the cosmos centre near the camp, where they would have looked at the night sky using huge telescopes that were two metres tall. Ms Tan had told the class they would see star clusters, craters on the Moon, and stars 17 000 light years away.

"There are no city lights out west," Ms Tan had said. "So the night sky is clear. It's magic, like sitting beneath a blanket of stars."

Now they wouldn't be doing any of this.

Chapter 2

Some Starry Ideas

"What will we do next week instead?" Toby asked, at last.

"Well, I still want us to have a fun week," said Ms Tan.

"How?" asked Toby.

"That's up to you," replied Ms Tan.
"I want you to work in groups and plan
fun activities for the class to enjoy.
We can do something different each day
of the week. And every activity should be
about – stars!"

It was nowhere near as good as going
to camp, but it was something at least.
The class started to plan.

Bella's group thought of making star-shaped pizzas for the class. Everyone liked that idea.

Ali's group thought of painting a mural
of stars and planets. "Maybe we could do it
on that big wall outside," Ali said.

Ty's group planned to show the huge size of the biggest star in the solar system – the Sun. "We can do that by marking out the planets around the Sun on the school oval," said Ty.

Scarlett's group decided on making stars
and planets to hang from the ceiling.
"We'll use balloons and cover them
with pieces of torn-up paper and glue.
Then we'll paint them," Scarlett said.

Toby's group, which included Luni, Blake and Ava, couldn't think of anything. They went home for the weekend, still thinking. By Sunday evening, Toby hadn't thought of a single idea.

Then, Toby heard something. His sister was playing the flute. She played the same tune, over and over. *Twinkle, twinkle, little star. Twinkle, twinkle …*

Toby had an idea.

Chapter 3

A Sparkling Show!

Toby told his group about his idea the next day.

"*Songs* about stars," he said. "We can sing!"

"But are there any songs about stars?" asked Blake.

It didn't take long to find out.

"There are *plenty* of songs about stars!" said Luni.

"And songs about astronauts and the Moon, too!" said Ava.

"We can learn the words, but none of us can play an instrument," said Blake. "What will we do for music?"

"Let's ask Mr Bell," said Ava.

Mr Bell was the school's music teacher. Toby's group went to see him and told him their idea of singing about stars.

"That's a great idea!" said Mr Bell. "I'll play keyboard for you, if you like. But it's such a good idea that I'd like you to perform for the whole school, not just your own class."

Toby thought performing in front of
the whole school sounded a bit scary.
But Luni, Blake and Ava were excited.

"We could dance as well as sing,"
said Luni. "We can make this wonderful!"

Luni and Blake made up some easy dance steps, and the whole group practised all week.

At the end of the week of fun activities, Toby's group performed for the whole school. They danced as they sang about wishing on a star, flying to the Moon, being under the Milky Way, walking on the Moon and a starman waiting in the sky. Toby even dressed up as a big star!

When the performance finished,
Mr Bell played the music from a famous
movie about a star-filled galaxy, and the
whole school jumped up and joined in
dancing. Everyone clapped and cheered
Toby's group.

They were – *stars!*